EMPIRE

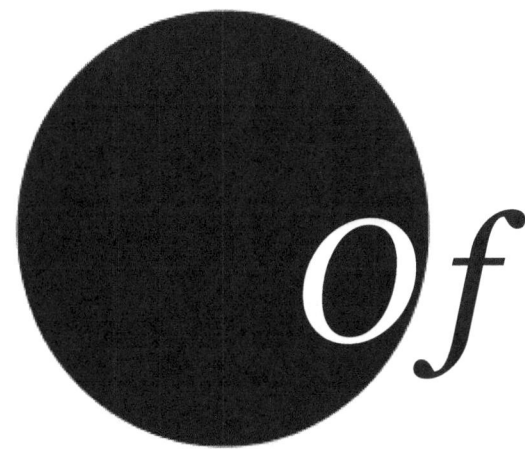

Of

SURRENDER

EMPIRE  of SURRENDER

Poems
Michael Schmeltzer

Wandering Aengus Press
Eastsound, WA

Empire of Surrender is the winner of the 2021 Wandering Aengus Book Award.

This book may not be reproduced or transmitted in any form by any means, electronic or mechanical, including photocopying and recording, or by any information storage and retrieval system, except for brief quotations embodied in critical articles and reviews. Excerpts may not be reproduced except when expressly permitted in writing by the author. Requests should be addressed to the author at mschmeltzer01@gmail.com.

©2022 Michael Schmeltzer
All rights reserved
First Edition | Poetry | Wandering Aengus Press
ISBN: 978-0-578-30841-8
Library of Congress Cataloguing-in-Publication Data available.
Printed in the United States of America

Cover Image:	"Resilient Weeds" by Dimitri Sirenko
	www.dimitriartist.com
Cover Design:	Meghan McClure
Author Photo:	L. Maria S.

Wandering Aengus Press
PO Box 334 Eastsound, WA 98245
www.wanderingaenguspress.com

Wandering Aengus Press is dedicated to publishing works to enrich lives and make the world a better place.

For my children—you are the word upon which I've built my world

CONTENTS

1	The Chronology of War
3	Feathers Where Fangs Should Be
5	War Like the Sting of a Honeybee
7	The Execution of *Goemon*
10	Pistil, Pistol, Honeysuckle
13	The Colonialist
14	In the City of No Children
15	About Farmers Forced to Harvest
17	Cure for a Horse on Fire
19	In the Land Where Fire is the Name of All Things
22	Stutter
24	Prosperity
26	After the War Parade, the Applause
28	Creation of the Empire
32	During the War We Become the Medium
40	A Sharpness of Axes
42	What You Do Not Shoot
44	They Eat Dog You Know
47	I am Blinking One Word Which is Now My World
51	And We Devour Our Own
55	Armor and the Fabulous Softness
58	Fragility is How We Survive
60	The Falling
63	To the Flawless Members of the War Tribunal
65	In the Great War I Become Cake

67	Antler by Antler Damage is Done
69	"are you ok I'm worried about You say something"
71	A Soft Rebellion
76	Kindness as a Kind of Weapon
77	Joy Apoptosis

Acknowledgments
Arigato
About the Press

EMPIRE Of SURRENDER

The Chronology of War

i.

First, a bullet
like the wrong word spoken.

Then, a battle
the people call civil.

Next, a boy
picks up a rifle, aims

at himself in a mirror,
and the reflection trembles.

ii.

First, the battle. No—first, a baby
betrothed to the bullet.

Then, a bomb. Then, the fields
decimated, the bulls

on fire, lighting a path through the dark
no one knew about.

iii.

First, a boy. Then, the bellow
of his father.

Next, the bells of the church
beatify the valley

which no longer grows
anything of note.

The boy looks to the steeple,
and among the villagers

he is the only one
who has not grown tired

of looking up, or listening
to the music of the Empire.

iv.

First, the many years of war.
Next, the news of the father's

return. First, the long battle.
Then, the empty bottles

lined up on the wall. Next, all the bullets shot
that went askew.

Next, the bullets that didn't.
A bottle shatters, and the boy watches

as his father takes aim, says nothing,
and pulls the trigger

as if the flash of the muzzle
could hold back the night.

Feathers Where Fangs Should Be

I know what I've done:
hammered out my fangs

and replaced them
with a celebration of feathers

in order to enamor, not puncture.
When threatened

every mouth should respond
with flight or flight.

Verily I learned to love
the rich

taste of blood
but only my own. How I've healed

is a mystery,
sponge-soft a nation as I am.

If children teach us anything
it's how to be weak

and better for it.
Don't believe me? Declare a war

you believe just;
I'll show you signatures

of good men on both sides

who claim for the sake of peace

we must tear out the tender
throats of children.

War Like the Sting of a Honeybee

Bury a mine
until the enemy is yours.

Watch as they step down
as if on a hive and shrapnel

rises like a swarm of bees.
Watch the bees

sink into the sovereign
flower of a soldier's body.

Search every bloom and bomb;
there is no honey

left in the world. I am peddling
dahlias and acorns, the auburn

of fat squirrels and the flit of finches.
No matter how handsome

deny the soldier who offers
a carnation in the age of carnage.

Don't be fooled into thinking the war
needs more red.

If heroism is the sacrifice
of self for others, what is more heroic

than the honeybee? Its sting

results in its death,

its abdomen eviscerated
in defense of the queen.

Dear Enemy, I am
no hero. I will do

no such thing for royalty.
Believe, I want to glory

in your suffering
but not nearly enough.

The Execution of *Goemon*

> Note: *Ishikawa Goemon* was a Japanese outlaw who stole valuables to give to the poor. He and his young son were publicly executed after a failed assassination attempt on a feudal lord.

The outlaw holds his young son above his head
to save the boy from boiling alive.

Or the outlaw holds his young son above his head
then plunges him in the boiling oil.

In all versions we need the father
to show us how to die

with arms uplifted as if in praise, as if he could
raise his child to paradise.

*

A riddle:
>Which version of this thief
>shows the most mercy?
>
>Which version of the son
>the heaviest?

A riddle:
>Who died first? The father
>who killed his son swiftly
>
>or the father who died
>knowing his boy was next?

*

In the great war a soldier's teeth
were battered from his mouth
for their gold crowns. In this way
he became monk-like, a vow of poverty

smashed into his face.

*

Because he died
experiencing such cruelty

he must have also known
enlightenment, a moment

of such clarity when relief
was all that was left

and all time became now
and all taste was blood and rice and soup his mother made

when he was sick and knew it would be
dinner time because no more

teeth or gold or sons or fathers, no value
in beating a dying man in a wrecked field

where oil and fire and men
bellow, armed to the teeth,

willing to gnash the bones of a father
for the sake of their sons.

*

Dear Deities of the Great War,
Emissaries of the Final Stillness,

before you belch up bombs and bodies,
I beseech you break my jaw

with the stock of your rifles
so I may know which words are most precious.

When I speak again it will be as one
who knows peace like an ache

of healing, like an arc
of a bullet

that misses its target.

*

When my father found the courage
to hold an immeasurable tenderness

in his hands, it was then he finally held
his grandson up.

Pistil, Pistol, Honeysuckle

i.

The night the child dreamt
an entire field of us

in efflorescence, he awoke
dizzy and wet, in love.

We swayed, we raised our arms
to swirl our scent. Such joy

we showed him.
Our bodies a spray of praise

which his limbs learned to mimic.
What dancing he does

now that he perceives
pleasure. O patriot

of petals, who could doubt
your loyalty? Eventually,

tragically, the boy follows
the bend at the edge of the forest

and turns traitor.
He buries the child

he was
in the blackest dirt he can find.

ii.

Somewhere a man plants a handful
of bullets

like seeds in the earth.
He grows body after body

until he can come home.
The honeysuckles stand at attention.

After tearing loose a handful
he brings a bundle

to his war bride.
And the groom weds

one white lash
to the woman's finger.

And the woman ties one lash
around the man's wrist,

then another, and another,
until it fools them

into believing his very veins
gush light

and bleed
an unbearably saccharine scent.

iii.

Dear Patriot of Petals,
 In your hand honeysuckles
  bound together with jump rope and lace.
Dear Love,
 In your hand honeysuckles
  bound together with more honeysuckles.
Dear Groom,
 In your hand honeysuckles
  bound together with your bride's hair and barb wire.
Dear War,
 In your hand honeysuckles
  bound together like prisoners to a pole.
Dear Torturer,
 In your hand honeysuckles
  bound together like cat o' nine tails.
Dear Tyrant,
 In your hand honeysuckles
  bound together like dissidents to more dissidents.
Dear God,
 In your hand honeysuckles
  bound together like nations by a border,

  one dying while the other cradles itself.

The Colonialist

Buried in rubble, a bloody child

claws her way to the surface

of bloody children.

*

A famous colonialist

once wrote in his journal:

> *I know the worth of the land*
> *based on how hard*
> *the young fight.*

In the City of No Children

Her open palm a map of panic.
        Beneath its surface a sewer of nerves
fevers the flesh. Flushed,

        the mother wipes her forehead
and calls out the name of her daughter.
        The name of her daughter

returns like leather
        to a slaughtered cow.
The mother claws the middle of her palm

        until blood like a divination
guides her onward. A thin dog
        tugs on a scarf

embedded in the ruins of a temple.
        Soon the black cloth rips, mimics
the sound of a struck match.

        Delirious, the mother spins
as if the sound of a fire lit
        was the plume of her child

        rising from the wreckage.

About Farmers Forced to Harvest

Do you remember the complex of crows
like a vacuum of space
sucking you into the courtyard?

You ran—a ridiculous willingness
to be swallowed whole—and the birds
burst upward, a reverse-demolition.

Our uncle once told us
about farmers forced to harvest
landmines in the war-torn fields.

How could we know
when the crows erupted
we were the threat?

We scrambled home,
fear like rotten milk on our tongues.
We hide like exiles

from our childhood
in a country not our own.
At the ash-end of life

we live like stolen money.
When my uncle was young
he had to wash the bodies

of dead soldiers
before they were shipped home.
Despite this, it was us

who hid our heads under a blanket
like seeds under soil.
It was us whose dreams

bore fruit, and we prayed
no crow's beak
would pierce

our skin,
no red pulp
would ooze from the pecks.

Cure for a Horse on Fire

In this war zone
a white horse

drenched in oil
is set on fire

by an arrow shot
from the opposite shore.

In this nightmare landscape
there is never a rider.

I am the archer
and the heart of the horse

beating itself,
trying to extinguish the flames.

*

What little I actually know
of equine and archery.

What little I know of fire
and what makes the heart pump.

An ex-lover swore fetishes
began in fear. It isn't the roar

of heat or the horse
that scares. It isn't the monster-shriek

of war. It's the river
I failed to mention in this retelling,

that cure
for a horse on fire.

How quickly it sweeps
animals downstream,

how efficiently the flame
is snuffed.

What little we know of love
and death

begins and ends
with limbs in a panic,

a hiss in the darkness like a torch
doused in that terrible rush.

In the Land Where Fire is the Name of All Things

Confess: when you first witnessed
the tranquil, blank page

of a dove's white wings,
all you wanted

was to scribble
the dark of the devil

upon them.

*

When the prince of the power of the air
sings the scales

onto every snake with such care
what else can it be

but a perverted hallelujah?
God sews each second

like a feather to our flesh
and yet we are not meant for flight.

We become time-laden.
We don't even wish

for sky. We grow tired and want
only to sit

until we're able to sink

deeper into dust from whence we came.

*

Those who study the dead world
know at the center of hell

is a patch of ash
the size of a hand

that the damned call 'heaven.'
Put your palm on it,

and it squeezes.
Place your cheek on it;

it caresses.
This, too, is hell.

In the land where fire
is the name of all things

even ash elevates itself
to the empyrean.

*

O sons and daughters of disobedience,
what you perceive as agony

is one aril of a pomegranate.
What you understand of peace

amounts to nothing more than a halo
around the throat of a hostage.

When the soldier was blinded
by a nearby landmine,

they said he cried black tears.
When asked what he remembered

he responded *god*
like a nova next to me

but the devil provided
every joule of heat.

Stutter

    before the bleat
               of panicked beasts

    before the blaze
                           of machine gun fire

        the brown goats

               chewed cud

               twitched their tails

        the kids too

               suckled and twitched

        the brown goats
                    riddled with bullets
        the kids too

               shudder under
brown heaps

and the soldier recalled

        the misfit he

               pummeled in school

        that farm boy who

               suffered seizures

                        that nailed him to

                the mud

                    the one

    with the hammering

                        stutter

                                who stammered

                                about killing

    chickens

                    this farm boy

                        whose wisdom came

                                from understanding

    chickens

                    look most alive

                            when flapping

their white wings

                                flapping

those angelic wings

                    as they elevated

            their headless bodies

Prosperity

The human tongue like the tail
of a scorpion—every word

first formed in the venom gland
of our brain.

The story about the scorpion
killing itself when surrounded by flames

isn't true. It's just dying,
despite the theatrics.

Was fire the first instrument
of torture

or was water? What we can do
with the simplest elements

is enough to keep me awake.
(Sleep, too, when taken away

is another form of punishment.)
And what about language well-wrought

and sadistic? We now define this
as a violence.

No...not define it. We make it
violence.

Not too long ago
we used music unbearably,

tortured our enemies with song.
Then we invented

a way to drown them
without drowning them.

I am at the grocery store
buying cotton candy grapes,

water in bottles, a honeycrisp
apple. I am stumped

by the number of body washes.
We're blessed with the privilege

of meandering up and down aisles
while listening to the heart-sick songs

of our youth
even though we're safely in love.

We forget the failures that matter most;
we call those moments

prosperity. We speak the boring platitudes
of peace

in order to keep moving,
and even during war we share

pleasantries as carefully
as shaking hands with a sword.

After the War Parade, the Applause

i.

A village that existed
mere seconds ago
disappears in a parade

of bombs. We celebrate wildly
while the villagers turn to

confetti.

ii.

A former soldier, now retired
school teacher, told me
once you become a father

every child is yours.
Even those dogs in detention.
The body of

a little girl, and next to her
the mother's shadow. I utter
the only prayer I can muster:

Children. Dogs. Detention.
Oh honey, I don't know
any other words for this.

iii.

Gunshots. Or

the sharp noise of my daughter
clapping her hands
when she sees me at the airport.

Both speak in a clipped accent,
but only one asks
a horrifying question.

I respond by crouching behind my luggage.

iv.

My daughter stops
clapping.

We are both terrified
of what will happen next.

v.

My wife thinks she knows
where to find beauty

so she kisses my calloused fingers,
caresses the sand-worn knuckles.

If she knew
what brilliance these hands

extinguished, she would cut them off
and burn them down to the bone

so no applause could ever be
released from them again.

Creation of the Empire

Day 1

First, god. Then, god.
Afterwards, all that is

not god.

Day 2

First, the trigger, the barrel, and the bullet
unite.

Next, the great war appears
like a lighthouse pointed at your face.

Then, a blast so bright it stains
our very shadows to the wall.

We burn with fever. We blister.
We amble toward water.

Day 3

First, the jackal
occupies the devastation.

Then, our outstretched hands
tempt his jaw

open
like a jack-in-the-box.

Next, a snarl—that curled thing
hiding in the mouth—viscous enough

for three wars.
Such dread. Such sacred,

powerful maw. O Menacing Beast,
Devil Dog, rust-colored

and ready to devour.

Day 4

The jackal in uniform
holds out his paw to a young girl

wandering the woods
as if offering directions.

She touches his claw.
Then, the curl of his lip. Then, the smile

and striptease of teeth, an expression
raw and naked

such as the girl had never seen.
Time behaves so strangely now;

this moment never ends.
They dance the wartime waltz

and no matter
what happens next, lullaby or lunge,

the child closes her eyes

and dreams of the Empire.

Day 5

First, a whimper. Then, a wound, the sound
of nations crumbling.

If you want to join the war effort,
pull the trigger.

If you want to join the Empire,
surrender.

Day 6

Peekaboo, says the child's skin,
        pale as a wedding veil.

Peekaboo, says the jackal,
        blushing with excitement.

Peekaboo, says the bullet,
        burying itself in the innocent.

Day 7

First—(guns)
And then…(gods)

Now the lighthouse, our shadows, and the great war.
Now the jackal, a child, and a trigger.
Now the world and the dead world. Now the Empire.

Peekaboo, says the Empire
        as we float downriver.

Peekaboo, says the Empire
        as the jackal spasms in delight.

Peekaboo, says the Empire
        as the girl howls, her mouth a sore full of song.

During the War We Become the Medium

Ears, for instance, pinned

to a belt, removed

from all hearing,

or bone from

an enemy's arm

carved into a letter opener.

Dear Mom & Dad,

■ don't know what they told you, but ■ okay and both pieces were removed and no major damage done. Nothing to do but rest in the hospital, the first good nights of sleep ■ had in months.

Tell the rest of the family not to worry. ■ tougher than ■ used to be.

Trench art: any decorative item

made by soldier, prisoner, or civilian

where the creation is directly linked

to armed conflict.

Dear Mom & Dad,

▮ held a baby for the first time. ▮ were told never to hold one, not even for a minute. Locals know ▮ the good guys. ▮ would bring them to the embassy if they abandoned them. ▮ held one because the mom's hands were full, and you raised ▮ right. When ▮ held the baby she stopped crying and the mom watched ▮ holding her little girl while she adjusted her bags and ▮ couldn't stop crying and crying even though the baby wasn't fussing at all. Then the mom took her, bowed, and left.

They have nothing here, and we're killing their sons.

What have we

undone? What could anyone

have possibly done

to require such art?

Dear Mom & Dad,

Give everyone a hug. Tell them ▮ going to be okay. Remember Matt, how he used to pick on ▮ dogs? ▮ wanted to punch that little shit sometimes. Imagining him rotting in a place like this kills me though. What ▮ wouldn't give to see his ugly face.

▮ pulled a gold tooth from a body. ▮ buddy says ▮ rich.

During the war

we become the medium.

Dear Mom & Dad,

You know how babies cry depending on what's wrong? ▓ *can translate the cries of the dying. Even the ones dying in another language.*

I can't stop hearing. Something's happening to ▓▓▓ *ears.*

Love,

▓▓▓▓▓▓▓▓▓▓

A Sharpness of Axes

I am soft. What of it? Like a blanket
that leaves the toes uncovered

I am what you might
consider not enough.

What weapon can be made of me?
I once was used to smother

a fire
but only a wick-sized one.

Oh sure, I have blazing ambitions.
I have the need to be on bodies

and useful. Better yet,
find me folded

on top of a stack of blankets.
I am tired

of people lately,
their mouths like two-way mirrors

and nothing of what they say
visible. Did you hear

the one about the tree
that walked steadfast into

a sharpness of axes?
This isn't a joke

but before chopping it down
the blades

they all laughed.

What You Do Not Shoot

A barefoot man, for instance,
wearing a crown of sweat

and holding a bucket of well water.
Or those who drop their rifles

then drop to their knees as if in worship
upon seeing the face of their destroyer.

And medics, too, no matter
how much gore

stains their uniforms. But of course
they were all targets,

their confusing insistence
on vulnerability

a thing violence
cannot tolerate. In school

we watched a video
of an antelope bounding away

in smaller and smaller leaps,
the lion closing the distance between them

and—
the whole class looked away but me.

What colors I saw.

There was a soldier in green

who shot a girl in the face
right in front of her mother

and then the mother soon after.
What he did not shoot

was their dog, the one whose masters
he had just killed

for he could not bear to stop
the yellow wagging of its tail.

They Eat Dog You Know

Yes, in the great war
we massacred dogs.

Afterward we ate them
roasted over fires.

Wag your tongues all you want.
We ate our enemies

and their families, too.
We ate the bamboo forests,

delicious as arrows
of asparagus, the mountains with teeth

like sticks of dynamite.
The shrines and the names

of all our dead digested
in our stomachs.

Limb by limb the nations
we swallowed. Judge us,

you and your kin
who have never been

this hungry.

*

I heard the joke about the Asian

restaurant serving canine,
the one about naming their kids

after the clang of utensils
thrown down the stairs.

It's only funny to Americans
who haven't watched

a starving father
use a chunk of flesh

to fish for dogs
who were also starving.

It's only funny if you don't
come home

empty-handed, chewing your child's name
like a piece of fat.

*

Stab our meat with a fork.
Call it hunting.

Put our chopsticks in your hair
and call it fashion.

We welcome you
into our homes. Opulent

obeisance, we've cooked
the most elaborate meal

you can't pronounce,
one you never had to call

sweetly to slaughter.

I Am Blinking One Word Which is Now My World

Note: While forced to participate in a propaganda video, POW Jeremiah Denton blinked the word "torture" in Morse Code.

Guards tortured the prisoner,
hung him from his wrists.

Later, he was forced
to kneel in gravel

until the skin was sheared
from his kneecaps.

Then, he finally gave them
the information they demanded.

My father, he confessed,
grows flowers.

*

I tell everyone
too much and right away:

about my kids
squabbling, my father's stroke

and the soft droop
on the half-moon

of his face.
I am over-familiar

and broken
so no need to deprive

or reward me. I'll tell you
everything I know.

*

If the prisoner blinked the one word
which is now his world

would it be *father* or *flower*?
If he blinked in Morse code

an entire universe into being
would it be one entirely cut

from the sharp edges of *shear*
or something else for which

there is no word for: the difference
between the sound of a seed

breaking through itself
and the sound of one

breaking between teeth,
the paradoxical calm of my mother's voice

when she called to say
my father wasn't feeling well

or the distress I felt when I found him
unable to move.

I lifted his sweat-soaked body
to the couch, told him I loved him,

we needed to call someone.
No, no, he said, and I,

both a good and terrible son,
disobeyed.

*

The guards paraded
the prisoners down the street

as the crowd pelted them
with the mush of rotten squash.

Unreasonably hungry as they were,
I imagine they tried

to catch with their mouths
anything they could stomach.

The mob lurched forward, punched and kicked.
Out of the eleven prisoners

tortured, all but one
returned home. What hurts

worse, the fact you wouldn't kill
the crowd of civilians

to save that one
or that you would? No one

is good. Is anyone good
enough to save?

*

They recorded the prisoner, asked him questions. He said:

> *I get adequate food and adequate clothing*
> *and medical care when I require.*

And while he spoke he blinked his eyes against the lights.
In Morse code he spelled the word *torture*.

That singular truth.

*

No, my father repeated,
the word stretching slowly from his mouth, pulled

from a part of the brain he could barely reach.
I walked away. I called for help. Unable to follow,

he blinked his panicked eyes. He blinked.
He blinked and blinked and blinked.

And We Devour Our Own

The wolf gives birth to more wolves
and gods detonate into more gods;

there is minimal miracle in that.
Dear enemies, my doe-eyed foes

from foreign lands, we will go
crazy, slowly,

then in a rush at once, together
like dancers in a musical.

War is the chorus
to the most popular song in the world.

Our lips move in unison.
We kick with metric precision

the nucleus
of a stranger's beautiful face

until it splits.
Who would have ever believed

melody
could stir us like that?

*

I watched a man for hours
shove an unpublished novel

into the shredder. Sheet after sheet
pushed itself into strips. He dipped his hands

in the trash like a ladle into noodles, absurd
in his eagerness and this

is how we die, thinking
we created something better from ourselves

when really
we bear gibberish and destruction.

*

A soldier shoots another in the head,
cavalier in his movements afterward.

I am not deranged; if you look at the photo
commemorating the moment

you'll see a dozen more soldiers emerge from the spray
like Athena erupting from Zeus, violence

a fully-formed heritage.
Remember what I said

about the man with the shredder?
It was me. I ate strip after strip

of paper, chewing
and making faces like a camel.

I watched myself in the mirror
and for a while I believed

it wasn't me doing what I watched
myself do.

*

My daughter asks me
what I'm looking at:

a building exploding
into jagged chunks of building,

a fanatic exploding into a red ecstasy
and still each piece

wants to keep killing. We keep repeating
the awful habit of cruelty.

We are hostage to sorrow.
Lay down. Rest your head.

We can be each other's pillow.
After a nap we can gnash

this wild world tender.
Then I will tell you

the story my mother told me
about a crane that hatched

a wolf, a divine act, and the pup,
in all its savage softness,

without hesitation,
ate the mother.

Oh no no, don't cry. It isn't too late.
I promise even that wolf

can be tamed.

Armor and the Fabulous Softness

The fabulous softness of chinchilla fur
is what caused the extinction
of one species, the two remaining

now endangered. We wear our lives
like a lavish shawl
we inherited and did

nothing to earn. We wear polished
armor to war and thick furs upon return
as if by covering our battle-mangled bodies

with the most vulnerable pelts
we could shield the stone fist of our heart,
which, if need be, we

would tear from our chest
and bludgeon our enemies with it,
crush their heads while children cower,

their soft, silken hair
offering
no protection either.

*

The baby rabbit,
whose white coat we are invited

to pet, trembles.
The yellow chick,

bright as a dandelion, shivers.
Be gentle, the volunteer warns us,

and the children at the petting zoo
who have gathered around

to hold something so helpless
even they have dominion over it,

they make of themselves
pudding, peach fuzz,

part sugar and full-fur.
You can stroke it

with the back of your hand,
the woman says, and the children do,

every one of them obedient
to the delicate.

*

The chick, a droplet of yolk.

The rabbit, that tiny god

of scrambling limbs. With two fingers

we can snuff them out like a match.

My god, our brutal and fragile

fires, these calloused hands

on my daughter's

incomprehensibly soft cheeks—

Fragility is How We Survive

Like a dandelion clock, for instance,
blown apart by a fox's breath;

that is how I've floated this far.
Not by anything other than gentleness

do I owe allegiance.
It worries me how many follow

the flight of an arrow
rather than the path of the pappus.

When the world confuses worship
and warship, all we can do

is sink. Even sailors are more
eggshell than coconut

but most nations remain
machete-minded. I am as dangerous

as an elegant spoon. I carry inside me
the same golden thing

even the most vile soldiers do.
Strike me down

if you don't believe. I break
myself too often

to prove
so much less.

The Falling

Sparrows built a nest
under the eaves of our house

so now I fear
the falling of little birds.

*

Another sad hiccup
of a fact: birds

eat birds. Why
should that bother me

when I see what we
are capable of? A prisoner

tortured, draped and hooded
like a crow, arms extended.

He stands on a box
and never takes flight. He dies

grounded.

*

Say *flightless.* Say *plummet*
as if it were a ripe fruit

and not the motion of red juice
dropping off my daughter's chin.

How do I explain the distance
between falling and failing

is negligible?
I can't keep catching her.

I know
the many ways we meet the ground.

I know wings
won't save us.

*

I had a friend
whose whole life rose

like the delicate throat
of a cormorant

snared around the neck,
her life sustained

by the smallest fish.
She loved pictures

of animals yawning, the jaws
opened not in violence

but exhaustion.
When she died I could not catch

my breath. I'm sorry;
I keep trying to tell you

something beautiful
about the way the birds now trill

outside my windows
but my sorrow chirps

urgent as hungry chicks.
Tell me

you hear the birds anyway.
Tell me you'll arrive

with food
falling from your mouth.

To the Flawless Members of the War Tribunal

I have, of course, hurt others
with the same hands I use

to wipe my father's
lopsided face.

The left half of his lips droop.
His mouth hangs open

as if about to speak.
I listen for my name.

*

Age melts the handsome
from him. He is wick

and from him I was born
wicked.

He cannot walk.
He cannot drink

the liquor he wants
so I give him water.

I decorate him
with a Nicotine patch.

Flawless members of the war tribunal,
while you deliberate

whether by match or torch
to raze my house,

my old life
suddenly burnt down.

In the Great War I Become Cake

Out of desperation I believed
in God

exactly four times
and each desperation

moves with me
like a sentimentality, like a piece

of trash my son once held
and hence I can't let go.

May I speak of the beloved
beetle I painted prismatic?

It opened itself like a ruby-colored gift
and dazzled a message

in multiple wings
but it never lifted. We can kill, especially

with our clumsy love. Friends,
how do we move

with the grace of kind words,
or like forgiveness we don't deserve

but receive? My prayer is to be more
ear and less tongue.

The more I witness the less I believe
I'm built for this world.

Growing up I willed myself
into a sword. Then as I aged

a shield.
I am old enough now

not to need war.
With each clang I hear the heart

quiet a little more.
In the great war I become cake.

I can't withstand
anything, not even a little rain.

I have one job; I feed the hungry
and refuse to ask

which side they slaughter for.

Antler by Antler Damage is Done

Think of the body as a museum
for experience; now all your wounds

are valued. Worn by weather and wrinkled,
I come to you

damaged. Of course, framed like this, I'm beautiful too
like antlers scraped and chipped

by other antlers.
What's unnatural is the untouched,

and friends, believe me when I say
many hands yoked me to my nature.

These scars like
an inconsideration of guests

overstay their welcome. Yet,
I invited each one; I am a gracious host

who makes the beds every morning,
sheets tucked so tight you could bounce

disappointments off them. Every night I jump
as if startled, jump on the beds and wonder

which parts of me stay, which parts will be repelled
like the ear to an off-key.

I have regrets. I'm full of discord

and ugly music. People reassure me, disagree

in their note-less ways; I'm not here
to argue but like the weakest among us

I wouldn't survive the smallest clash.
Look to the deer at war, percussive

and clack-happy. Not even animals in battle
do I cheer. When I witnessed the world

celebrate
the infamous terrorist

shot,
I flipped over on my back and sobbed.

"are you ok I'm worried about You say something"
—SPAM *email subject line*

I am burning crayons in the dark.
Have I returned to

or destroyed my
childhood? Every color

melts, especially our favorites.
Who once said their bones

were as soft as candle wax?
Those with ears

listen. Those without ears
listened too much. I heard

it takes
eight pounds of pressure

to rip off the human ear
and an immeasurable amount

of willpower. Keep listening.
Please

worry. I lost
so much.

A father arcs a chainsaw
down on a rosebush

then pats himself on the back,

a demolition of blossoms.

A mother approaches
with a pair of hand shears

and sculpts the damage done,
says to the clueless man, "yes, yes, dear, you *are*

one of the good ones."
What the father knows of pruning

amounts to a squirrel-head more
than he knows of love.

He twitters like the smallest bird
with the biggest beak. He speaks

but does not hear. He places
garbage in the garbage

but tenderly
as if it were precious.

We have misplaced our gentleness.
Mothers, fathers, listen.

Some of us hurt
others while some of us hurt.

We have taught the young
how to

tear flesh
with their baby teeth.

A Soft Rebellion

with a nod to Gerald Stern's "Lucky Life"

Exactly a year after my father's stroke, a butter-yellow bird
flew into the window near where I was reading.
I went out and cupped it the way a child would
catch rain in his hands
thinking eventually he could
quench his thirst, that optimistic
and hopeless.

*

Tradition states when eating the ortolan
you must cover your head in a towel.
Shield from God's eyes
the decadence and shame of such
sin. To eat music itself while remaining
in silence and darkness.

*

I stroked the bird back to consciousness.
When I put it down it couldn't fly;
it hopped and hopped. What happened next
is awful and happens
to all of us, though the method varies.
I don't want to say it yet.
For now please understand everything
I do wrong I do
out of a stupid desire
to be good.

*

The bird is to be consumed whole,
feet first, while the person holds
the head.

*

I am ready to tell you
the way one may eat the ortolan
is the way the drain consumed the bird
as it skipped away in fear.
Feet first, then the egg drop of its body.
Finally, the delicate head
disappearing, that final, lovely thing.

*

Intelligent disobedience—the trait
in service dogs to ignore commands
if it goes against the safety
of their owner.

Father, Bird, give me an order
so I can prove my love.

*

"You're creating beauty, Henry"
an old man said to an even older man
over cups of coffee.
I wasn't brave enough to ask
what it was Henry did. I don't know
if I ever asked
a brave question but friend,

pretend I did ask, and the older man
said he made leaves of red glass and wire
that hung from his porch and when the wind blew
they made a tiny music, small as the song
of a bird you could hold
in the palm of your hand.

It is beautiful, isn't it? Leaves
that never fall, glass that never mistook itself
for air.

*

Dear Bird,

The old man talked about his father who owned a barbershop and the lime-scented aftershave all the men requested. There's beauty in that, too. To use a straight razor and leave the skin smooth. To understand a blade doesn't always harm. Another man he knew was shot for brandishing a knife. He didn't talk about birds or glass or sky. He didn't mention death. He just shook his head when he said the police shot the man. He knew the man wasn't a threat; he would have listened if told to put down the weapon; he would never have disobeyed.

*

Dear Old Man,

My father can't walk anymore. He doesn't speak about his father like you do, and I don't know what my grandfather did for a living, or how he used his hands. I inherited his machete from the war. My father knew a few men who shot others, and men who had been shot. Unlike you, he isn't a storyteller; what he knows he mostly keeps to himself, an egg of memory, careful not to crush or reveal it. He will die with the whole egg in his mouth, and I will be there to wipe his lips after. Is it the recognition of beauty or the failure of it to cry over the death of a bird I once held in my palms? I did not want to hurt it so I put it down. What do I know of caring for the broken, or about stories like this?

*

When my father suffered a stroke
he repeatedly mumbled
not to call 911.
I could not obey.

I left the living room
and talked to the emergency operator.
I described his sloped face, his paralysis
and slurred speech
"like words on top of other words,"
my daughter said.

I walked back in.
I waited for the EMTs
to lift his limp body and drive him to the hospital.
I comforted my crying mother. I called my wife.
I waited again.

My father. My mother.
Nurses, doctors, janitors, strangers,
cooks and cashiers—
everywhere I walked and waited
for someone to acknowledge how I ignored
my father's single, urgent command,
my soft rebellion.

*

Dear Bird,

I heard a story on the radio about a truck
that nearly collided with a blind man.

Dear Old Man,

The man's dog held him back
despite the stern order to proceed
and saved the life of this new father
and the infant daughter he had strapped to his chest.

Dear Stroke,

You've taken too much.
All I ask in return
is to hear
the relieved father say
good boy, oh good boy,
oh good good boy. Good boy.

Kindness as a Kind of Weapon

So often my name has played
on the lips of those who hate me

I must be their magnum opus,
a musical made

by those who confuse the barrel
of a rifle with the body

of a flute. What music they create
echoes in the emptiest halls

and yet they bow as if vitriol
needed a soundtrack.

And if such animosity can be
a kind of music, then I have crafted

kindness
into a kind of weapon

you can swing with one hand
like a foam sword

from a state fair.
Here, children, snatch it from my hand.

Beat me again and again
until you're satisfied.

Joy Apoptosis

When I wake I drop
my death like a bomb

from the highest mount I know.
Then I begin my day

whistling. The way cream
swirls light into coffee, the way sugar

sweetens while disappearing…
this is how I blend myself

into my children.
I'm growing old. War

repeats itself on the news
but I managed to surrender

my fear.
I set every last sadness ablaze

the way soldiers
burn the huts they raid.

Now I'm extinguished
by a maple-dark exhaustion.

I've left my family
nothing in my will

but joy like a pinwheel
spinning. I tuck my children in.

I kiss their heads as I would
kiss this ravaged world, tenderly

as pushing a pin
back into a grenade.

Acknowledgments

The author wishes to thank the editors of the following periodicals in which some of the poems, occasionally in a different form, were first published:

Anti-Heroin Chic	"Kindness as a Kind of Weapon"
	"To the Flawless Members of the War Tribunal"
Book of Matches	"Armor and the Fabulous Softness"
cream city review	"Cure for a Horse on Fire"
Jack Straw Writers Anthology	"The Colonialist"
	"Feathers Where Fangs Should Be"
Los Angeles Review	"After the War Parade, the Applause"
Michigan Quarterly Review	"Prosperity"
	"'are you ok I'm worried about You say something'"
Moria	"In the City of No Children"
The Night Heron Barks	"Fragility is How We Survive"
The Pinch	"In the Great War I Become Cake"
Pleiades Magazine	"The Execution of *Goemon*"
Superstition Review	"A Sharpness of Axes"
Tupelo Quarterly	"They Eat Dog You Know"
	(reprinted in Jack Straw Writers Anthology)
Water~Stone Review	"The Chronology of War"
	"Joy Apoptosis"

Arigato

Theo and Sophiana: In a world full of swords, always choose to be cake. I love you both and am so proud of you two. Thank you for this life of immeasurable softness and defiant joy. Without you, there is no peace.

Lydia: Thank you for loving me through every wound until I could be my better self. You teach me everything I need to know about kindness, grace, and forgiveness. I love you to the end of every empire.

Meghan: Thank you for being both shelter against and witness of the slings, arrows, etc, of all my outrageous misfortunes. You are the ideal reader I write toward, always.

Miss Rosie: You have been a most unique and surprising source of delight during a time I needed it most. Thank you, dear friend, for every kind letter, every colorful bird.

Jane, Kelli, and Kevin: Thank you for teaching me, through the example of your poetry, how to be the writer this book needed. I am indebted to each of you. Thank you, over and over, for your generous, insightful attention.

Thank you to the Jack Straw Cultural Center, especially Levi Fuller, Joan Rabinowitz, and Kathleen Flenniken, for honoring me with a Writing Fellowship during which some parts of this book were written.

Thank you to those who continue to show kindness in an age when cruelty and dehumanization are rewarded as righteousness. Thank you to the cruel; through you I know myself better. This book is for all of you.

And last, but not least, thank you to the team at Wandering Aengus Press for giving this book of tenderness and brutality a home.

About the Press

Wandering Aengus Press is a small, literary press with a growing list of poetry, fiction, and nonfiction. We publish books that bring the joys as well as the injustices of the human experience into vivid focus. We are dedicated to publishing works to enrich lives and make the world a better place.

Learn more at www.wanderingaenguspress.com.

Winners of the Wandering Aengus Book Award

Michael Schmeltzer — *Empire of Surrender* (poetry)

Alina Ștefănescu — *dôr* (poetry)

Tarn Wilson — *In Praise of Inadequate Gifts* (memoir in essays)

Kevin Miller — *Vanish* (poetry)

www.ingramcontent.com/pod-product-compliance
Lightning Source LLC
Chambersburg PA
CBHW072016290426
44109CB00018B/2257